Please don't squeeze your boa, Noah!

Marilyn Singer • Pictures by Clément Oubrerie

Henry Holt and Company • New York

To Brenda and Simone
—M. S.

To Grumblu
—C. O.

Acknowledgments

Thanks to Steve Aronson. —M. S.

I'd like to acknowledge the influence of the following artists:
David Hockney, Marcel Gotlib, Gary Larson, Red Grooms,
Ralph Steadman, and Saul Steinberg. —C. O.

Henry Holt and Company, Inc. / *Publishers since 1866*
115 West 18th Street / New York, New York 10011

Henry Holt is a registered trademark of Henry Holt and Company, Inc.

Published in Canada by Fitzhenry & Whiteside Ltd.,
195 Allstate Parkway, Markham, Ontario L3R 4T8.

Library of Congress Cataloging-in-Publication Data
Singer, Marilyn.
Please don't squeeze your Boa, Noah / Marilyn Singer; pictures by Clément Oubrerie.
Summary: A collection of poems on a wide variety of animals, including common
pets as well as dolphins and wet chickens.
1. Children's poetry, American.   2. Animals—Juvenile poetry.   [1. American poetry.
2. Animals—Poetry.]   I. Oubrerie, Clément, ill.   II. Title.
PS3569.I546P57   1995   811'.54—dc20   94-12847

ISBN 0-8050-3277-0
First Edition—1995
Designed by Clément Oubrerie
Printed in the United States of America on acid-free paper. ∞
1   3   5   7   9   10   8   6   4   2

The art for this book was done in a combination of acrylic, pastel,
ink, and color pencils on various kinds of paper.

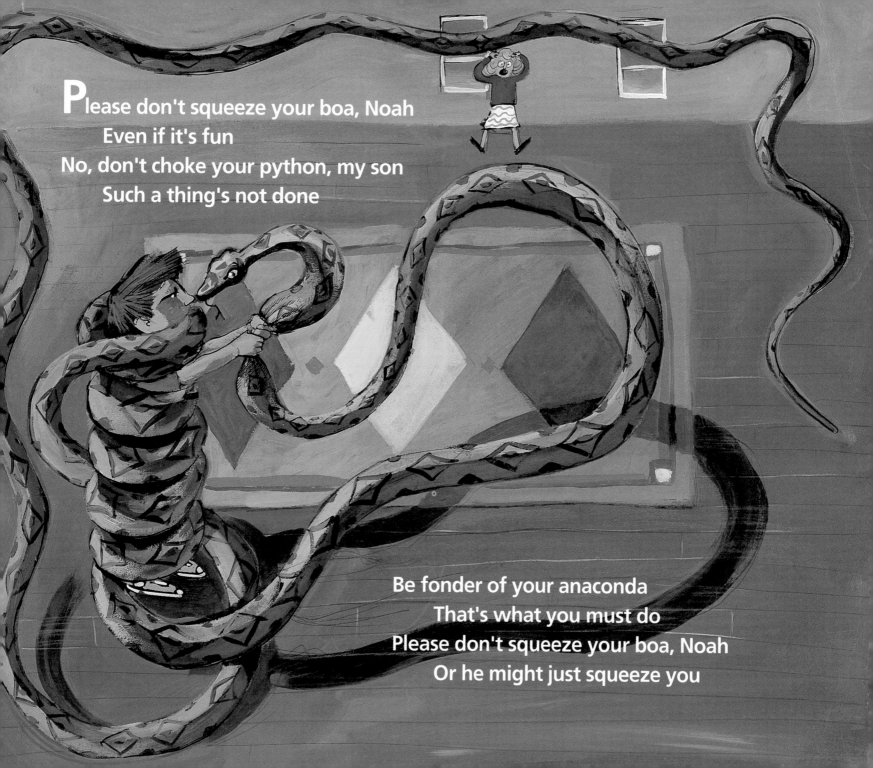

Cats walk tiptoe on their paws

They'll learn to use a litter box

They'll sleep curled up on dirty socks

Cats act like they have seen a ghost

They'll use your couch for a scratching post

and never show the slightest shame

They seldom seem to know their name

nature's laws:

No cat will wag a friendly tail

No cat will answer his fan mail

Cats hunt birds and mice and fishes

They clean their plates, but don't wash dishes

Catnip makes cats quite enthused

But if you laugh, they're not amused

Remember that your guppy
is a fish and not a puppy
You can't kiss it, you can't hug it
You can't take a leash and tug it
You can't walk it to the bank
You must leave it in the tank
It won't gaze with soulful eyes
It won't win a fancy prize
It can't give you fleas or rabies—
just a lot of guppy babies

A bath will make a pooch upset
So will, of course, a shower
A drizzle's bound to make him fret
A storm to make him cower
So tell me, is it just a whim
That dogs hate water but love to swim?

Tricky treat
　　my parakeet
mimics noises from the street
　　Her siren's great
Her horn's first rate
　　Her school bell warns you don't be late
Her tire squeal
　　is very real
Her car alarm is one big deal
　　What a pity
if we left the city
　　She'd start sounding like a bird—
and that's much too pretty!

A frog is fond of puddles

A pig enjoys her mud

A catfish wants a little pond
complete with slimy crud

A camel — if you've got one —
can stand the open sky

But a chicken in the rain'll want to cry
'cause a chicken's much more happy when it's dry

A hamster likes his wood chips

A dove a nest of twigs

**A lizard loves a mound of sand
that it can call his digs**

**A cockroach —if you've got one—
will take what he can get**

**But a turtle in the dirt'll surely fret
'cause a turtle's much more happy when it's wet**

Why is Fido barking?
Who can ever tell?
Is it some loud banging?
Is it some odd smell?
Why is Fido barking?
Did he see a cat?
Does he hate the flowers
on your grandma's hat?
Why is Fido barking?
Did you make a face?
Did he see some Martians
land from outer space?
Why is Fido barking?
Does he want to run
Is it 'cause he's thirsty?
Or is it just plain fun?

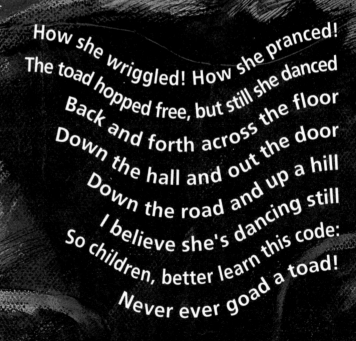

Ginger Jenkins liked to tease
Tommy Tenkins's toad Louise
She dressed it up in ballet clothes
and made it spin upon its toes
One day Louise seized the chance
and jumped right into Ginger's pants
How she leaped and how she twirled!
How she shimmied! How she whirled!

How she wriggled! How she pranced!
The toad hopped free, but still she danced
Back and forth across the floor
Down the hall and out the door
Down the road and up a hill
I believe she's dancing still
So children, better learn this code:
Never ever goad a toad!

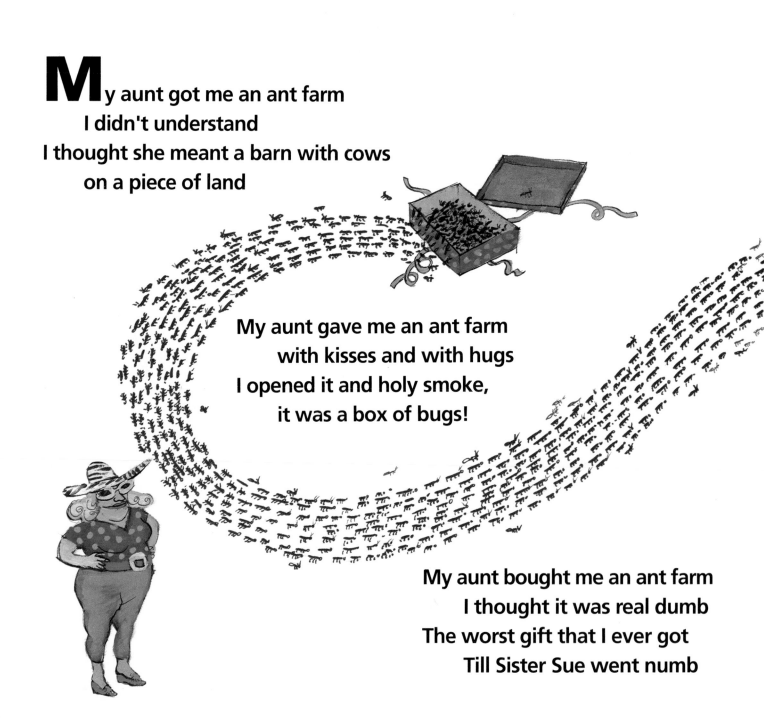

My aunt got me an ant farm
I didn't understand
I thought she meant a barn with cows
on a piece of land

My aunt gave me an ant farm
with kisses and with hugs
I opened it and holy smoke,
it was a box of bugs!

My aunt bought me an ant farm
I thought it was real dumb
The worst gift that I ever got
Till Sister Sue went numb

The brat stared at my ant farm
And then she got quite frantic
"I have to move away," she yelled
"This place is much too ant-ic!"

My aunt got me an ant farm
O rapture, joy, and bliss!
Now my ants and me share harmony
in my room without Sis!

A

A tree-climbing feline named Brown
Got stuck in a tall maple's crown
Twelve large firemen
Three clowns and one hen
All helped the scaredy-cat down

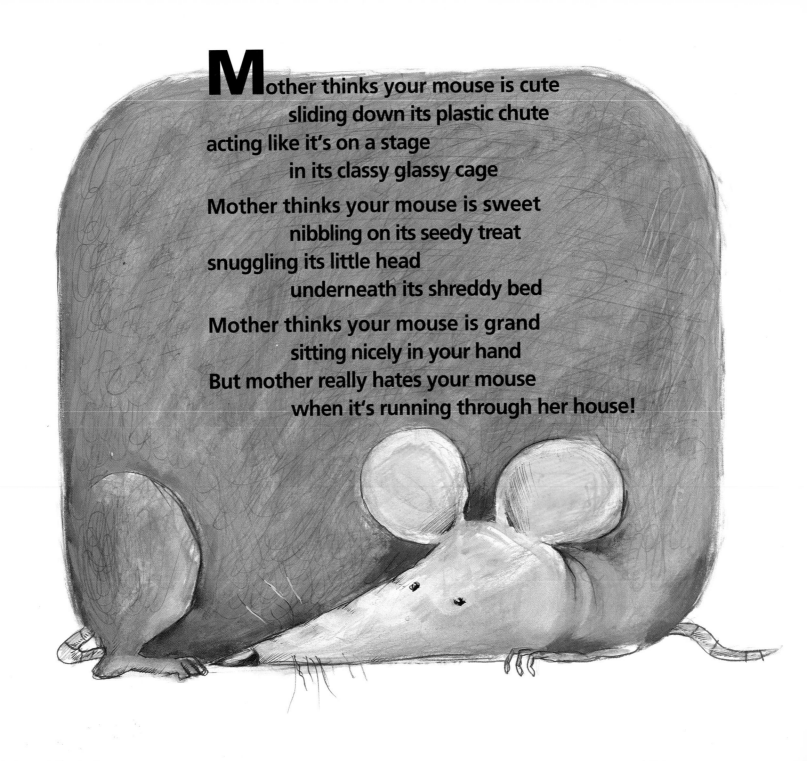

Mother thinks your mouse is cute
    sliding down its plastic chute
acting like it's on a stage
    in its classy glassy cage

Mother thinks your mouse is sweet
    nibbling on its seedy treat
snuggling its little head
    underneath its shreddy bed

Mother thinks your mouse is grand
    sitting nicely in your hand
But mother really hates your mouse
    when it's running through her house!

Magilla is a fussy cat
He dislikes this, he dislikes that
He doesn't care for sirloin steak
or lobster tails or chocolate cake
I offered him some caviar
He turned his nose up at the jar
A bowl of milk won't please Magilla
He will eat ice cream — just vanilla
Fancy tidbits I keep buying
Tempting morsels I keep trying
Magilla treats them with disdain
That puss is driving me insane!
What does he like to lick or chew?
What will he eat — I've got no clue!
But stranger still is how that cat,
So picky picky, stays so fat!

Birds make whistles, chirps or caws

Some can speak, but they can't spell

Birds don't have a sense of smell

All our feathered friends lay eggs

All of them have got two legs

All birds have wings (or sometimes flippers)

None of them are good with zippers

f nature's laws:

 An eagle flies, an ostrich walks

No bird has teeth (not even hawks)

Some birds are shy, some birds are trusting

Some eat food that's just disgusting

 Some birds will let you pet and kiss them

Some are gone before you miss them

Here's my spider, big and hairy
Do you think she'd be less scary
If I said her name was Mary?

Pretty Mrs. Quivers
        likes pets that give you shivers
Tarantulas and big brown rats
        Scorpions and vampire bats
Rattlesnakes and slimy slugs
        Cockroaches and water bugs
Toothy eels and glaring vultures
        Great white sharks and germs in cultures
Snapping turtles with bad breath . . .
        But bunnies frighten her to death

I wondered if I'd ever get
an eating, sleeping, real-live pet
instead of just some old stuffed toys
'cause Pop said pets make too much noise

Puppies howl

Kittens mew

Grizzlies growl

Pigeons coo

Piglets oink

Monkeys hoot

Bullfrogs boink

Finches flute

Horses whinny

Brown bats squeak

Dolphins squinny

Parrots speak

Then Mom came up with the solution
    to keep us safe from noise pollution
She said we could adopt a newt
    It's kind of cute — and also mute
So now we live in harmony
    Mom and Pop and Newt and me

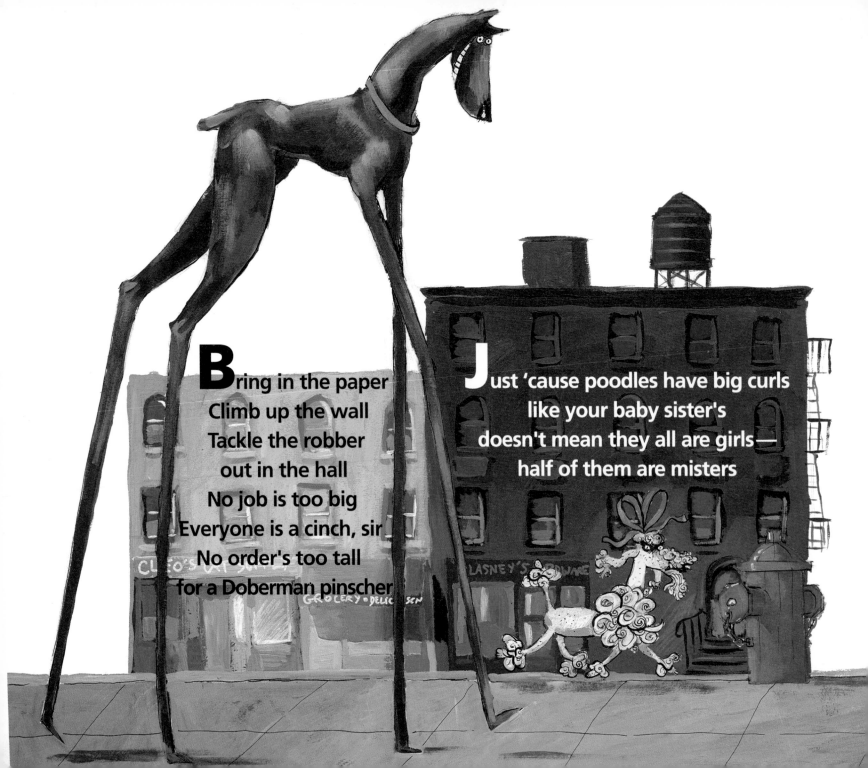

Bring in the paper
Climb up the wall
Tackle the robber
out in the hall
No job is too big
Everyone is a cinch, sir
No order's too tall
for a Doberman pinscher

Just 'cause poodles have big curls
like your baby sister's
doesn't mean they all are girls—
half of them are misters

The greyhound has a famous habit
He dearly loves to chase a rabbit
In the woods and all around
At the track or underground
If he's made a big mistake
And finds his quarry's just a fake
He doesn't care
To him it proves
A rabbit's anything that moves

I know a man named Mr. Spats
     who has at least one hundred cats
Cats on the table
     Cats on the floor
Cats on the sofa
     Cats by the door
Cats in the pots
     Cats in the pans
Cats sleeping on the tomato soup cans
     Kitties in the bathtub
Felines in the sink
     Pussies on the TV set that's always on the blink
It's hard to visit Mr. Spats
     with all of his one hundred cats
You have to watch out where you're sittin'
     or you might plop down on a kitten

Dogs cannot pull in their claws

Dogs have to pant to get real cool

or else jump in your swimming pool

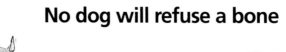

No dog will refuse a bone

or ever use a telephone

Dogs can frolic by the ocean

but never need your suntan lotion

nature's laws:

 In the grass they're good at flopping

but not so hot at grocery shopping

 Dogs can untie your shoelaces

and fill up lots of empty spaces

 Dogs can learn to give their paws

and appreciate your kind applause

Tell a secret to your rabbit
And he certainly won't blab it
It's just simply not his habit